CW00431990

ISBN: 9798654496898

For Abbie,
Thank you for the many hours putting the world to rights, when the world was a funny place
Love, Nicky and Brian xx

Acknowledgements

Having spent nearly twenty years working with children and young people, books and stories have played a huge part in all aspects of my career. From sharing stories in nurseries, to researching lessons as a lecturer, to studying the way that books are created in my degree. Books are such special things, they have a magical ability to allow us to lose ourselves in their pages, to feel like we are at one with the characters and find resolution in their storylines. My love of books has been one which spans years, and some of my favourites still sit on my book shelf. In 2014 I left my full-time teaching post and told my tutor group that I would dedicate my time to developing my book collection, which had sat as an idea in notebooks for so long. On the arrival of Brian, my real-life cockapoo, in 2015 the dream just became more and more real. I am delighted to be able to share the Adventures of Brian with families and bring the magic of books and the wonders of therapeutic storytelling together to offer a combination of stories and support to children. Before we start this special story, there is thanks to be given;

To my Mum and Dad, who have given me the encouragement to move forward with a dream of creating stories to help small people. Thank you for standing by me, encouraging me and sharing these precious moments.

To Richard for your belief and encouragement that there was a set of books inside me that should be written, this shiny diamond is very grateful.

To my nan and grandad, who forever guide me to follow this path that I am on and to ensure that I stay true to my dreams.

To Veronica and Brian, eternally in my heart, you inspired the little fluffy boy who became the centre of these books and shared so many precious memories.

Finally, to all our friends who have supported us, encouraged us and inspired us in the development of the Adventures of Brian, we are so grateful for your love each and every day.

I hope you enjoy these books as much as I have enjoyed writing them

Love Nicky x x

THE ADVENTURES OF BRIAN

HELPING CHILDREN OVERCOME THEIR FEARS AND WORRIES

This book belongs to:

....

Brian was lying on the sofa looking out of the window when he heard his mummy's keys rattling. It could only mean one thing – walkies!

Brian leapt off the sofa, ran around in a circle and let out a bark of excitement. He loved walkies! It was his favourite thing! He grabbed his favourite squeaky ball and hopped into his harness, before leaping out of the door.

As he trotted along the path with his mummy, Brian sniffed the air and enjoyed the breeze ruffling his fur. It was a beautiful sunny day and he felt so happy!

As they wandered towards the park, Brian felt the excited feelings grow in his chest. He LOVED the park. He pulled on his lead to make his mummy walk faster, and as soon as his paws touched the grass he rolled and rolled and rolled. Soon, Brian was covered in grass and waiting for his mummy to throw him his ball!

As his mummy unclipped his lead Brian became so excited that he ran super-fast in circles around her. His mummy laughed at him as he ran round and round in circles before coming to a stop in front of her.

Brian waited impatiently for his mummy to throw his ball. He was so excited now that he could not sit still. He fidgeted and wiggled on the spot waiting for her to throw.

As the ball flew through the air, Brian ran after it as quickly as he could. As he picked it up he ran back to his mummy and flung the ball at her feet. Brian was so happy. He ran after his ball, again and again.

As he played with his mummy, Brian saw his friend Benson coming across the field. He waited for his mummy to say it was ok, before trotting over to say hello. Benson wagged his tail as they greeted each other.

"Morning Benson!" Brian said as he greeted him. "Hi Brian! What are you up to?" Benson replied! Brian showed Benson his ball, "playing ball with my mummy!" Brian told him, his tail wiggling so fast! "Do you want to play?". Benson nodded and they ran to play together.

As they played with the ball, Brian and Benson laughed, barked and rolled in the grass together. However, after a while, Benson stopped sharing and kept running off with Brian's ball. Brian felt the cross feelings growing in his tummy. It was his ball and he wanted to play with it too, Benson was not doing nice sharing!

Brian tried really hard not to get cross, but every time Benson ran off with his ball and would not give it back, he felt the angry feelings growing.

Brian tried really hard to stay calm…. but the next time Benson ran off with his ball, his angry feelings exploded and he barked and barked at Benson, telling him off for taking his ball.

Brian's mummy picked up Brian's ball, clipped on Brian's lead and told him it was time to go home. Brian did not think it was fair, he was sharing, Benson was not!

When Brian got home, he felt sad and cross with Benson. He did not think that it was fair that he had to come home. Benson was being unkind, Brian had been trying to share his ball! He wandered into the garden and flopped on the grass with a big 'huff'.

Blue Butterfly saw Brian flop on the grass and floated down, worried about her friend. "Hi Brian, what is the matter?", she asked softly.

Brian looked up at her and started to cry.

He told her about trying to share his ball, and that Benson had run off with it. He told her about the angry feelings, and how he told Benson off and that his mummy made him come home to calm down. Blue Butterfly listened quietly.

When he finished, Blue Butterfly gave him time to take a big breath, "Brian, it is very hard when our friends do not share, and it is even harder when they take our things". Brian nodded, "it made me very angry, and I did not like the feeling" he told her. Blue Butterfly nodded.

"When other people do things that make us feel uncomfortable, or break the rules, it can make us feel very angry. It is not nice when other people do things that make us feel sad" she agreed. Brian looked up at her, "why did Benson do it?".

Blue Butterfly sat on her flower. "Brian, sometimes, people do not realise that their behaviours really hurt us. Do you think Benson was trying to make you angry? Or was he just too excited when he was playing and forgot to share?", she asked.

Brian thought about it, Benson did not seem to be trying to hurt him, and he knows how excited he gets sometimes. Sometimes, he is so excited to play ball he forgets to give it back to nanny and grandad as he is having so much fun. "Maybe he was excited?" he whispered.

Blue Butterfly nodded. "Brian, sometimes, other people get so caught up in their own feelings that they upset us and do not even mean to. Next time, instead of barking and getting angry, you could use your words and tell Benson that he is upsetting you, if you cannot solve it you could ask an adult for help".

Brian thought about this. He had been so angry with Benson that he had not used his words at all. He had just felt the angry feelings getting bigger and bigger and bigger – then he had got really cross!

Brian thought about the day. If he had told Benson that it was making him upset, Benson might have shared his ball. Then he would not have gotten so angry.

Or, he could have asked his mummy for help and she could have got his ball and they could have played chase instead. Then he would not have had to come home early.

Brian looked at Blue Butterfly. "Those ideas would have worked better than getting angry" he told her.

Blue Butterfly smiled, "Brian, it can be really hard when we get angry. But, if you had told Benson at the start that he needed to share, or changed your game, then your angry feelings would have disappeared instead of getting huge" she explained.

Brian nodded, Blue Butterfly was right, she always had good ideas.

The next day, Brian was in the garden playing in his paddling pool when he heard Billy, the dog next door, start to bark. Billy had a really big bark!

At first, Brian was too busy playing to take much notice of all the noise that Billy was making, but soon, his head started to hurt from all the noise.

Billy barked, and barked.
Billy barked really loud!
Billy's bark got bigger and bigger....

Very soon, Brian started to feel the angry feeling in his body creep upwards. He did not like the noise. It made his head feel too busy and it started to make him feel very angry.
Brian stood very still, he did not think he could put up with the noise Billy was making for very much longer. He thought about what Blue Butterfly had taught him.

Why might Billy be making so much noise?
Was Billy ok?
Who could help Brian to stop the noise in his head making him so angry?

Brian ran indoors to his mummy and hit her knee with his paw. As she looked at him Brian ran to the fence and barked to her.

Brian's mummy came outdoors and stood still, Billy was still barking.

Billy barked, and barked.
Billy barked really loud!
Billy's bark got bigger and bigger….

Brian's mummy looked at Brian, she ruffled his head. "Good boy Brian, let's find out what is wrong with Billy shall we?". Brian jumped up to give her a hug, before his mummy popped her head over the fence and talked to Billy. Brian tried to listen but his mummy's voice was very quiet, but he did hear say, "that's what is the matter!".

Brian's mummy jumped down and picked up the telephone. He heard her call Billy's mummy on the phone. There were a lot of 'ahhs' and 'ooos' and when she put the phone down, she told Brian "we need to go and help".

Welcome

Brian's mummy put on his lead and they left the house, when they got to Billy's house, his mummy met them at the door.

Billy's mummy explained that the door to the garden was stuck. Billy was in the garden and she could not let him in. Brian stopped and thought. So, Billy was making all that noise to tell them that something was wrong. Billy was scared and that was why he barked so much!

Brian felt so pleased that he had told his mummy instead of letting the angry feelings take over, it meant that they could help Billy feel safe again. Brian knew that when we do not feel safe we can get very scared and angry – that must have been what was wrong with Billy!

Before long, Brian's mummy and Billy's mummy had fixed the door and Billy came bouncing into the house. Brian was so happy his friend was ok, and they played and bounced together!

As they sat in the garden together, Billy turned to Brian. "Thank you for getting help for me Brian" he told him.

Brian smiled, "I am glad that I remembered to ask an adult for help Billy. At first all your barking made me feel really cross as it hurt my ears".

Billy nodded, "I did not know how to tell people I was stuck?" he replied. Brian looked at him carefully, "you must have been very scared?" he asked. Billy nodded again, "it was really scary Brian, I did not like it and I started to get angry feelings as no one was helping me", he shared.

Brian thought about everything he had learnt about angry feelings. He realised that we all get angry for different reasons, but we need to learn what the feeling is like and get help to make them feel better. "I am glad that I listened to your barks instead of getting angry too" Brian whispered.

That afternoon, they ate ice lollies and played in the garden together making happy memories.

As Brian went to bed that night, he felt very proud that he had learnt so much about angry feelings.

Brian knew that when he got angry, the feeling started creeping in from his tummy and got bigger and bigger. Blue Butterfly had helped him realise that he did not have to let it explode, he could choose to ask for help instead.

Brian knew that he could choose to use his words to tell people how he felt.

Brian knew that if he could not make it better, he could ask an adult to help him.

Brian knew that if we do not feel safe it can make us panic and feel angry, so we need to ask for help to get to a safe place again.

As he fell asleep, Brian felt proud that he had learnt to make his angry feelings smaller so that he could have more fun every day.

THE ADVENTURES

OF BRIAN

HELPING CHILDREN OVERCOME THEIR FEARS AND WORRIES

Other books in this series:

Brian and the Blue Butterfly

Brian and the Magic Night

Brian and the Black Pebble

Brian and the Christmas Wish

Brian and the Shiny Star

Brian and the Naughty Day

Brian and the Funny Feeling

Brian and the Poorly Day

Brian and the Big Black Dog

Brian and the Scary Moment

Brian and the Proud Feeling

Brian and the Sparkly Rainbow

Brian and Boo's Big Adventure (Special Edition)

Brian and the Changing Path

Brian and the Christmas Sparkle

Brian and the Night-time Noise

Brian and the Rescue Pups

Brian and the Forever Family (Special Edition)

Brian and the Troubling Thoughts

Brian and the Kind Deeds

Brian and the Christmas Box

Brian and the Honey Bees

Brian and the Shaky Paws

Nicky lives in Sussex with Brian the Cockapoo where they enjoy daily adventures with friends and family. Nicky started her career by spending 10 years working in the early years sector with 0-5 year olds before lecturing in early years and health and social care to students aged 16 and over. She later retrained as a hypnotherapist and now runs A Step at a Time Hypnotherapy working with children and adults to resolve their personal issues.

The Adventures of Brian books were the development of a dream of wanting to offer parents of young children tools and resources to support their children to manage worries and fears in a non-intrusive way. Having spent a large part of her career reading stories at all speeds and in all voices this collection of storybooks was born.

Each book in the collection covers a different worry which affects children on a day to day basis and uses therapeutic storytelling to support children in resolving these through Brian's daily adventures.

You can find more titles in the Adventures of Brian series by visiting:

www.adventuresofbrian.co.uk

Printed in Great Britain
by Amazon

56360019R00020